SEX EDUCATION and PUBERTY BOOK FOR BOYS 8–12 YEAR OLDS

Essential Guide to Raising Sexually Informed Boys in the 21st Century

By

Cory Silver Smith

Cory Silver Smith

TABLE OF CONTENT

INTRODUCTION

I can't wait to guide you through the fascinating realm of sex education.

I understand your possible reaction: "Ugh, do we really have to talk about this stuff?" But rest certain that this will be an entertaining and educational ride.

Imagine studying everything there is to know about your own body as if you were embarking on an expedition to explore a new continent.

You may be pondering the significance of sex education. Well, for starters, being curious about your body and your sensations is very natural and normal.

As you become older, knowing how your body functions and how to make wise decisions about your relationships can help you feel more self-assured and empowered.

Additionally, sex education teaches students how to respect one another, communicate effectively, and maintain their health and safety in addition to teaching them about sex.

All of them are crucial life skills that you will find useful whether you're interacting with close friends, relatives, or love relationships.

What can you anticipate from this book, then? We'll cover a lot of ground, I suppose. We'll start by going over the fundamentals of your body's operation. We'll discuss puberty and all the alterations it brings.

We'll delve into creating wholesome connections, including effective communication and boundary-setting techniques.

Additionally, we'll discuss gender and sexual identity and how to support people who may identify in a different way than you.

Of course, we'll also go over the specifics of safe sex and hygiene so you can maintain the health and happiness of your body.

Don't worry, though; this won't be like a dull health lesson. Along the way, we're going to have a good time. Quizzes, games, and even some corny jokes will be included.

And don't be hesitant to ask if you have a query or don't understand something. Keep in mind that the main goal of this book is to give you knowledge and confidence about your body and your relationships.

Are you prepared to start this trip, then? Let's get going!

CHAPTER ONE

Importance of Sex Education for Boys

Let's first discuss what sex education is in reality. Even though we will undoubtedly address the mechanics of sex, it's not just about that. Understanding your body, your feelings, and your relationships are important.

It's about gaining the skills to successfully communicate, set limits, and make decisions that will keep you safe and in good health.

Now, some individuals could believe that girls should only receive sex education. After all, it's usually women that become pregnant. Wrong. Boys, understanding your bodies and your relationships is just as important to you as it is to girls. This is why:

It helps you make informed decisions.

You may choose what you want to do (and what you don't want to do) better when you are aware of the dangers and negative effects associated with various sexual actions.

With this information, you'll be able to safeguard your partner and yourself from unintended pregnancies, STIs, and other health hazards.

It teaches you about consent and respect.

Sexual relationships should always be based on mutual respect and consent. By learning about what consent means and how to communicate effectively, you'll be better equipped to have healthy, positive relationships with others.

It empowers you to take control of your own health.

Sex education isn't just about sex – it's also about understanding your body and how to take care of it.

By learning about hygiene, contraception, and other aspects of sexual health, you'll be able to stay healthy and happy throughout your life.

It helps you build healthy relationships.

Relationships are about more than just sex – they're about communication, trust, and respect. By learning how to communicate effectively and set boundaries, you'll be better equipped to have positive relationships with friends, family, and romantic partners.

It promotes gender and LGBTQ+ equality.

Sex education isn't just for straight, cisgender people. By learning about different gender identities and sexual orientations, you'll be able to be an ally to your friends who may identify differently than you.

You'll be able to challenge harmful stereotypes and stand up against bullying and discrimination.

So, boys, are you starting to see why sex education is so important? It's not just about learning how to put on a condom (although we'll definitely cover that too). It's about understanding your body, your emotions, and your relationships. It's about empowering you to make informed decisions and stay healthy and happy. It's about promoting equality and respect for all people, regardless of their gender or sexual orientation.

So let's dive in and explore this awesome world of sex education together!

Goals of the Book

Okay, let's get into the goals of this book! But first, let me ask you a question: have you ever played a sport without knowing the rules or the goal?

It's difficult to play a game when you don't know what you're attempting to accomplish. The same is true for sexual education. That is why we will discuss the book's objectives.

Our initial goal is to assist you in understanding your body. That's right, we're talking about your entire body, from your head to your toes (and everything in between). We'll go over what each part is for, how it looks, and how it operates.

"Why do I need to know this?" you may wonder. So, if you understand what's going on down there, you'll be better able to care for yourself and communicate with others about what feels good and what doesn't.

Our second purpose is to assist you in comprehending your emotions. Sex is about more than simply physical pleasure, believe it or not. It's also about feelings, such as love, attraction, and want. We'll go over how to recognize and express your emotions in a healthy manner.

You will be able to create stronger and more rewarding relationships with people once you understand your emotions.

Our third purpose is to assist you in better understanding your relationships. Even for adults, relationships can be challenging.

You may, however, develop healthy connections with friends, family, and love partners by learning about communication, respect, and limits.

We'll also discuss consent: what it is, how to obtain it, and how to offer it. You will be able to have positive and respectful sexual experiences if you understand consent.

Our fourth purpose is to assist you in comprehending the world around you. The world is a huge place with a lot of various kinds of individuals. We'll discuss diversity, which includes diverse genders, sexual orientations, and cultures.

You will be able to form meaningful connections with people who are different from you if you appreciate and respect diversity.

Our fifth and last goal is to make sex education enjoyable and interesting! Let's face it: discussing sex might be unpleasant or uncomfortable at first.

But it doesn't have to be that way! We'll utilize delightful and engaging exercises, games, and real-life examples to make learning about sex education enjoyable and engaging.

So, those are the goals of this book: to help you understand your body, emotions, relationships, and the world around you, as well as to make sex education enjoyable! By the end of this book, you will have a solid foundation of knowledge and abilities to make informed decisions and build healthy relationships. Are you ready to get in and begin learning? Let's get started!

How to Use this Book
Welcome to the section on how to use this book! You might be thinking, "I know how to read a book.

Why do I need instructions on how to use it?" Well, this book is a little different from your average novel or school textbook.

We want to make sure you get the most out of it and have fun while you're learning. So, let's go over some tips on how to use this book effectively.

Tip 1: Read it with an open mind

The first thing you should do when using this book is to approach it with an open mind. You might hear things you've never heard before, or things that challenge your existing beliefs or ideas.

That's okay! The point of sex education is to learn and grow, so keep an open mind and be willing to learn new things.

Tip 2: Take breaks

Learning about sex education can be a lot to take in, so don't be afraid to take breaks. You don't have to read the whole book in one sitting. Take a break when you need to and come back to it when you're ready. Maybe even grab a snack or go for a walk – it's all about finding what works for you.

Tip 3: Use the interactive features

We've included plenty of interactive features throughout the book, like quizzes, games, and thought-provoking questions.

Don't skip over these – they're designed to help you engage with the material and make learning fun. Plus, they'll help you remember the information better.

Tip 4: Talk to someone

Sex education can be a sensitive topic, and you might have questions or concerns that you don't feel comfortable discussing with your parents or guardians. That's okay! You can talk to a trusted friend, teacher, or healthcare provider. They can help answer your questions and provide support.

Tip 5: Take action

Sex education isn't just about learning – it's about taking action. Use what you've learned to make informed decisions about your body and your relationships.

Speak up when something doesn't feel right or when you're not sure what to do. Remember that you have the right to make your own choices and set your own boundaries.

So, there you have it – some tips on how to use this book effectively. Keep an open mind, take breaks, use the interactive features, talk to someone, and take action. By following these tips, you'll be well on your way to becoming a sexually informed young boy!

CHAPTER TWO

Understanding Bodies and Reproduction

Welcome to the Understanding Bodies and Reproduction chapter! This is a crucial chapter since it serves as the foundation for all else you will learn about sex education. This chapter will discuss the various elements of the body and how they work together to create life.

We'll also look at some prevalent misconceptions about bodies and reproduction, as well as debunk a few myths along the road. So, let's get started!

First and foremost, let us discuss the various body parts. Some of them, such as the arms, legs, and head, are presumably familiar to you. But what about the reproduction-specific components? These are the penis, testicles, and prostate gland in boys.

They are the vulva, vagina, uterus, ovaries, and fallopian tubes in females. Don't worry if you've never heard of some of these; we'll go over them in greater depth.

Let us now discuss how these components interact to create life. This is where replication enters the picture. Reproduction is the process of creating new life, and it is primarily comprised of two components: sperm and eggs.

For guys, sperm is generated in the testicles, while for girls, eggs are produced in the ovaries. When sperm and egg combine, they can form a fertilized egg, which can develop into a baby.

But wait a minute, reproduction is more than just sperm and eggs. Hormones are also substances in the body that assist regulate processes like puberty and fertility.

The major hormone for boys is testosterone, which is responsible for muscle growth, voice deepening, and the growth of facial and body hair.

The major hormones in girls are estrogen and progesterone, which are responsible for breast development, menstruation, and pregnancy.

Let us now discuss some prevalent myths regarding bodies and reproduction. One of the most common myths is that males and girls are fundamentally different and cannot achieve the same things.

This is simply not true! While there are certain distinctions between boys and girls, such as reproductive areas of the body, there are also many activities that both boys and girls can perform.

Sports, music, art, and a variety of other hobbies can be enjoyed by both boys and girls.

Another widespread myth is that only women become pregnant. While it is true that girls carry babies throughout pregnancy, it takes two to make a baby: a sperm and an egg. As a result, boys play a significant part in reproduction as well!

So there you have it - the fundamentals of human bodies and reproduction. We've discussed the many elements of the body, how they interact to create life, and some prevalent misconceptions and myths.

Remember that it is normal to have questions and to not know everything. Keep an open mind, and we'll talk more about sex education in the next chapters.

QUIZ TIME

1. What are the parts of the body specific to reproduction for boys? A) Arms and legs

B) Penis, testicles, and prostate gland

C) Vulva, vagina, and uterus

D) None of the above

2. What is reproduction?

A) The process of creating new life

B) The process of aging

C) The process of learning new things

D) None of the above

3. What is the main hormone responsible for things like muscle growth and deepening of the voice in boys?

A) Estrogen

B) Progesterone

C) Testosterone

D) None of the above

4. True or false: Boys and girls are completely different and can't do the same things.

A) True

B) False

Answers:

1. B) Penis, testicles, and prostate gland

2. A) The process of creating new life

3. C) Testosterone

4. B) False

Basic Anatomy of Male Body
Understanding the fundamental anatomy of male bodies is an essential component of sex education for males. To avoid confusion and unneeded worry, it is critical that individuals understand their own bodies and how they function. In this

chapter, we'll look at the basic anatomy of male bodies and how they function.

The penis, testicles, prostate gland, scrotum, and urethra are all elements of the male body. Understanding these components and how they interact is essential for boys to feel at ease in their own bodies.

Let's start with the penis, which is the male reproductive system's exterior portion. It is divided into three sections: the root, the shaft, and the glans.

The penis root is linked to the pelvic bone and includes the erectile tissue that assists the penis in becoming erect. The shaft is the penis's long, cylindrical component, while the glans is the penis's rounded tip.

The testicles, or testes, are two tiny organs that hang in a bag beneath the penis called the scrotum. The testicles are in charge of creating sperm as well as the hormone testosterone, which is required for male growth.

The prostate gland is a tiny gland located near the bladder that produces the fluid that transports sperm during ejaculation.

The urethra is the tube that connects the bladder to the penis and transports urine and sperm out of the body.

Now that we've reviewed the fundamental anatomy of male bodies, let's look at how these elements interact to produce new life. When a boy hits puberty, his body begins to generate sperm in the testicles. The penis grows erect during sexual excitement, and semen is expelled from the body by ejaculation.

Semen is a fluid-containing mixture of sperm and fluid from the prostate gland and other glands.

It is critical to remember that everyone's body is unique, and there is no such thing as "normal" male genitalia size or shape.

The size and form of the penis vary naturally, and it can alter in size and appearance over a person's life.

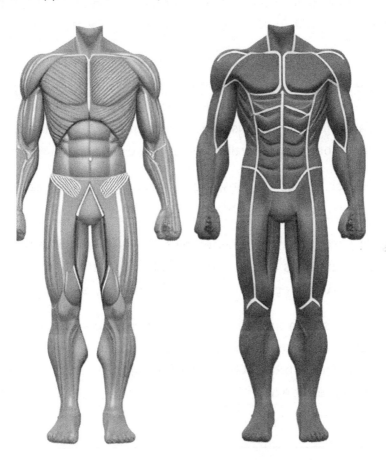

It's important for boys to feel comfortable with their own bodies and understand that everyone's body is different.

Learning about the basic anatomy of male bodies is an essential part of sex education, and it can help boys feel more confident and informed about their own bodies.

How Reproduction Works

Understanding how reproduction works is a critical component of boys' sex education. It is critical to understand how the male and female reproductive systems collaborate to create new life. In this chapter, we will look at the reproduction process and how it works.

The male reproductive system produces sperm, which is required to fertilize the egg of a female. During sexual contact, sperm is ejaculated from the penis and travels up via the vagina to the fallopian tubes, where fertilization can take place.

The ovaries, fallopian tubes, uterus, cervix, and vagina comprise the female reproductive system.

Eggs are produced and released by the ovaries and pass through the fallopian tubes and into the uterus. The uterus is the location where a fertilized egg implants and develops into a fetus.

Millions of sperm are expelled into the female's vagina when a male ejaculates during sexual intercourse. Sperm travels through the cervix and into the uterus, and if an egg is present, one of the sperm may fertilize it.

After fertilization, the fertilized egg implants in the uterine lining and begins to grow.

It is critical to understand that not every sexual encounter results in fertilization.

The time of ovulation, the quality and quantity of sperm, and the presence of any reproductive disorders are all factors that can influence the chances of conception.

It's also critical to realize that not all fertilized eggs result in a pregnancy. Fertilized eggs do not always implant in the uterus, and the pregnancy may end in miscarriage.

It is important to remember that there is a season for everything; there is a time to develop, a time to marry, and a time to give birth; and to make the most of your life, you must plan ahead of time and ensure that you arrive at the appropriate age and moment...

You must ensure that you achieve in life and become a better person before marrying and having children in order to care for your wife and children. THIS IS MY KIND OF SECRET.

Finally, understanding how reproduction works is an important component of sex education for guys. It is critical to understand how the male and female reproductive systems interact to create new life.

Boys can develop a better awareness of their own bodies and how they function in connection to the opposing sex by learning about the reproductive process.

.

In the next chapter, we will discuss how to maintain healthy relationships and communicate effectively with others about sex and reproduction.

What happens during puberty

Puberty is an important time in the life of a boy. It is the time when the body goes through a lot of changes, both physically and emotionally, as it grows from childhood to adulthood.

It's critical for guys to understand what happens during puberty so they can prepare for and manage the changes.

Puberty normally begins between the ages of 8 and 12. During this phase, the body starts producing hormones that cause physical changes.

The most visible difference is the growth spurt, during which boys can grow several inches taller in a short period of time. As males acclimate to their new bodies, their fast growth might make them feel awkward and clumsy.

Other bodily changes occur alongside the growth spurt. Boys' faces, underarms, and genital parts will begin to acquire hair.

As their vocal cords lengthen and thicken, their voices will begin to deepen. Boys may develop acne as their skin becomes oilier due to an increase in sebum production, a natural oil generated by the skin.

Boys may begin to experience more complicated emotions as they hit puberty.

They may be self-conscious about their changing bodies and feel pressure to conform to their classmates' expectations. It's critical to reassure guys that puberty is a natural process that everyone goes through.

Encouraging children to express their emotions and providing a secure and supportive environment will help alleviate the emotional turbulence that might occur during this time.

The development of the reproductive system is another key alteration that occurs throughout puberty. Boys will have their first ejaculation, which can be perplexing and even frightening. It is critical to explain what is going on with their body so that they do not feel embarrassed or ashamed.

Boys may begin to have sexual attraction to others during puberty. During this time, it is critical to discuss healthy relationships, limits, and permission.

Boys can be helped to manage their emerging feelings and wants by encouraging open communication and emphasizing the necessity of respecting themselves and others.

To summarize, puberty is a period of tremendous change and growth for guys. Understanding what happens throughout puberty might help them prepare for and manage the changes.

It is critical for parents or caregivers to offer a safe and supportive atmosphere and to foster open communication so that boys can ask questions and express their feelings. The necessity of safe sex practices and contraception will be discussed in the following chapter.

Quiz Time

1. What age range do boys typically experience puberty?

a) 4-6 years old

b) 8-12 years old

c) 16-20 years old

d) 30-40 years old

2. What is the most noticeable physical change during puberty?

a) Hair growth

b) Voice deepening

c) Increase in height

d) Acne

3. What is the first sign of puberty in boys?

a) Growth spurt b) Facial hair growth

 c) Deepening of the voice

d) Testicular growth

4. What is the term used to describe the first ejaculation?

a) Puberty spurt

b) Wet dream

c) Ejaculatory reflex

d) Male orgasm

5. What emotional changes can boys experience during puberty?

a) Anxiety and depression

b) Increased self-confidence

c) Decreased emotional sensitivity

d) Lack of interest in socializing

ANSWERS

1. b) 8-12 years old

2. c) Increase in height

3. d) Testicular growth

4. b) Wet dream

5. a) Anxiety and depression

How to deal with my changing body

Hello there, young man! Are you ready to discover one of the most exciting - and occasionally awkward - aspects of growing up? We're talking about puberty, the period in your life when your body begins to change in exciting (and occasionally odd) ways.

So, what changes can you anticipate? To begin, you may notice that your voice begins to sound different. It could creak or break, or it could suddenly become extremely deep - like, Darth Vader deep! Don't be concerned; it's all part of the process.

You may also notice that you are becoming taller and that your physique is beginning to change. Your arms and legs may appear longer, and your clothes may no longer fit as well as they once did.

You may even become clumsy at first, as you adjust to your new physique.

Let's chat about your private bits while we're on the subject of new body parts. Yes, we're referring to your penis and testicles. They begin to grow and change during puberty, which can be strange at first. But don't worry; this is quite normal and happens to every boy.

As your body changes, you may begin to experience new feelings. You could be happy one minute and irritated the next.

You may feel shy or self-conscious, especially in the presence of other individuals your age.

You may also develop sentiments for persons you find attractive, such as crushes or even a girlfriend or lover.

All of these changes can be overwhelming or even frightening, but trust us when we say that they are all part of growing up. If you have any questions or concerns about your body or your feelings, talk to a trusted adult, such as a parent, teacher, or doctor.

They can help you understand what's going on and provide the support you require to feel confident and at ease with your changing body.

So, prepare ready for an exciting trip since puberty is only the beginning of all the fantastic things your body can do!

Consider yourself a tiny seed that has just been planted in the dirt. You begin as a tiny little thing, scarcely visible to the human eye. However, as time passes, you begin to grow and change.

Your stem begins to spread upward, yearning for the sun. Your leaves begin to unfold, absorbing nutrients from the dirt. You might even start to develop colorful and flavorful blooms or fruit.

That's similar to what happens during puberty. You begin as a small boy, a germ of a person. But, like a plant, you begin to develop and alter over time.

Like a stem, your body extends taller and stronger. Like leaves, your muscles and bones grow bigger and stronger. And, like flowers or fruit, your private parts begin to expand and mature.

But, like a plant, growing up can be difficult at times. You may believe that you are not growing quickly enough or that you are expanding too quickly.

You may be self-conscious or embarrassed about your appearance. However, you are not alone in this process, just like a plant. You have caring parents, teachers, and other people who want to see you grow into a healthy, happy young man.

So keep evolving, adapting, and asking questions. You're on your way to becoming a fantastic, fully developed human being!

CHAPTER THREE

Building Healthy Relationships

As you become older, you'll develop a variety of relationships with the people around you. You'll have friends, family, instructors, coaches, and possibly a crush or two. However, not all relationships are equal. Some can be beneficial and healthy, while others might be toxic and detrimental.

So, what constitutes a healthy relationship? Here are a few things to remember:

Communication: Good communication is the foundation of any healthy relationship. That means listening to each other, speaking honestly and respectfully, and working through problems together.

Respect: You should always treat others with respect, no matter who they are or what they've done. That means listening to their opinions, valuing their feelings, and treating them the way you'd like to be treated.

Trust: Trust is essential in any relationship. You need to be able to rely on each other, keep promises, and respect each other's privacy.

Boundaries: It's important to set boundaries in any relationship, whether it's with a friend, family member, or romantic partner. That means knowing your limits and expressing them clearly, and respecting other people's boundaries as well.

Fun: Healthy relationships are also enjoyable and fun! You should be able to have a good time with the people in your life, whether you're playing sports, watching movies, or just hanging out.

But how do you actually build healthy relationships? Here are a few tips:

Be yourself: The best relationships are built on honesty and authenticity. Be true to yourself, and you'll attract people who appreciate and respect you for who you are.

Listen: Remember, communication is key! Listen to what others have to say, and show that you care about their thoughts and feelings.

Practice empathy: Try to put yourself in other people's shoes and understand their perspective. This can help you build stronger connections and avoid misunderstandings.

Be open-minded: Everyone is different, and that's what makes the world interesting! Keep an open mind and be willing to learn from others, even if they're very different from you.

Have fun: Remember, healthy relationships are also enjoyable! Don't forget to have fun and make positive memories with the people in your life.

By building healthy relationships, you'll not only create a positive and supportive environment for yourself, but also make the world a better place. So go out there, be kind, and make some awesome new friends!

Understanding Emotions and Empathy

Have you heard the expression "put yourself in someone else's shoes"?

It's a term that signifies attempting to understand how someone else feels by imagining yourself in their shoes. Understanding and sharing someone else's feelings is what empathy is all about.

It might be difficult to grasp how another person feels, especially if we have never experienced the same situation. But it doesn't mean we can't give it a shot.

Paying attention to how other people react to situations is one method to cultivate empathy.

Someone who is crying, for example, may be sad or distressed. Someone who is smiling and laughing may be joyful or thrilled. We can begin to grasp how someone else is feeling by paying attention to these clues.

Another key aspect of empathy is the ability to demonstrate our concern. This can be giving someone a hug, a nice remark, or simply listening to them when they need to talk. It's not always necessary to tell someone that we're here for them.

But what about our feelings? It's also crucial to recognize and express our own emotions. It's normal to feel angry, depressed, or annoyed at times.

We can express our feelings to someone we trust, such as a parent, teacher, or friend. They could be able to provide assistance and make us feel better.

31

It's also crucial to understand that everyone's feelings are unique. Just because someone else does not react in the same manner that we do does not make their sentiments any less valid.

Even if we don't entirely comprehend how someone else feels, we can cultivate empathy by being kind and supportive.

Role-playing with a friend or family member is a fun approach to cultivate empathy. You can take turns pretending to be someone else and envisioning how they might react in a given situation.

This can help you develop empathy while also being a pleasant exercise to conduct with someone else.

Remember that empathy is a valuable quality to have in life. It assists us in developing healthy relationships and better understanding the world around us.

So, the next time you talk to someone, put yourself in their shoes and observe how you feel. You might be amazed at how much empathy can teach you and help you grow.

Here's a fun story to help illustrate the concept of empathy:

Tim was a tiny boy who lived once upon a time. One day as Tim was headed to school, he noticed his friend Mike crying on the pavement. Mike had tripped and scraped his knee, which was bleeding.

Tim was concerned for his friend and wanted to make him feel better. He was aware that when he received a scrape or a cut, it hurt a lot and made him miserable.

So Tim sat down next Mike and wrapped his arm around him. He apologized for injuring Mike and said he understood how he was feeling.

Mike looked up at Tim once he had stopped crying. He grinned and thanked him for his friendship. Tim was pleased that he could make Mike feel better.

Tim made it a point from then on to constantly look out for his pals and show empathy when they were down.

He realized how vital it was to attempt to understand how people felt and to offer support and comfort whenever they needed it.

Types of relationships (friends, family, romantic)

Have you ever heard the expression "No man is an island"? That's because humans are social beings that enjoy forming connections with others.

We build all types of relationships throughout our lives, from playground friends to family members we see at holiday feasts to the special someone we might meet someday.

Let's start with friends - aren't they the best? Friends are people who share your interests and can make you laugh till you cry. They're the people you turn to when you're down, and they'll always have your back.

But did you realize that it's also crucial to work on your friendships? You must be a good listener, communicate your feelings, and be truthful. Remember that you receive back what you give!

Family is a little different from friends in that you can't actually choose them. Your family loves you and wants what's best for you, even if they can drive you crazy at times. Even if you don't always agree, show them some love and respect.

Then there's romance...we know it's not on your radar right now, but it's still vital to learn about! When you develop feelings for someone special, you may want to spend more time with them and get to know them better.

It is critical to be patient and honest with yourself and with others, as well as to respect their sentiments.

As an example, consider a soccer team. We all have many types of connections in our lives, just like a soccer team.

Family relationships are analogous to team members. Your family members are the ones who will always have your back, just as your teammates do on the field.

They inspire you to achieve your best and cheer you on, just like your family members do for you in whatever you do.

Friendships are analogous to the spectators in the stands. Your friends are the people who come to cheer you on from the sidelines.

They may not be on the field with you, but they are an essential member of your squad.

Romantic relationships are analogous to the coach. A love partner can be someone who supports and inspires you to be the best you can be, much as the coach directs and advises the team.

They may not be on your squad, but they are still significant in your life.

Remember that, just as each player on a soccer team has a certain function to play, each relationship in your life is distinct and valuable in its own right.

Whatever type of relationship it is, it is always necessary to put forth some effort to make it work. You must speak with one another, listen to one another, and demonstrate that you care.

And who knows, you might just make some of your fondest memories with the people with whom you form these relationships!

Consent and boundaries

It's critical to grasp the principles of consent and boundaries in partnerships. Simply said, consent is the act of giving permission, while boundaries are the act of establishing limits.

"But I'm just a kid!" you may be thinking. "Why should I care about consent and boundaries?" The truth is that you have the right to say "yes" or "no" to things that make you uncomfortable, even at a young age. It's also critical to respect other people's rights to say "yes" or "no."

Let us begin with the idea of consent. Everyone participating in an action or situation has given their consent. This could range from playing a game with friends to hugging someone.

anything's not okay to do anything if everyone concerned hasn't agreed to it. For example, it is not acceptable to push your friend to play a game that you have suggested.

It's critical to remember that just because someone doesn't say "no" doesn't imply they agree. It's critical to pay attention to what they say and their body language. If they appear uneasy or reluctant, it's better to inquire if they're okay with what's going on. And if they say "no," you must respect their decision.

Let us now discuss boundaries. Boundaries are the restrictions we place on ourselves in order to feel safe and comfortable. It's okay to say "no" to activities that push your boundaries, even if other people are fine with it.

It's okay to say "no" and propose a different game if someone wants to play a game that makes you uncomfortable.

It is also critical to respect the boundaries of others. If someone says "no" to anything, it's crucial to listen to them and not force them to do it anyhow.

Consider how everyone has a "bubble" surrounding them when thinking about consent and boundaries. This bubble symbolizes our personal space and boundaries.

It is acceptable for individuals to approach our bubble, but it is not acceptable for them to break it without our permission. It's also not right for us to burst someone else's bubble without their permission.

Remember that understanding consent and boundaries is a critical component of developing successful relationships. It is never too early to begin learning about them!

Quiz Time

1. What is consent?

a) When someone is forced to do something they don't want to do

b) When someone agrees to something of their own free will

c) When someone changes their mind after initially saying no

2. Is it okay to pressure someone into doing something they don't want to do?

a) Yes, if it's something you really want

b) No, never

c) Only if they eventually agree

3. What should you do if someone says no to something you want to do?

a) Keep asking until they say yes

b) Respect their decision and find something else to do

c) Try to persuade them to change their mind

4. How can you tell if someone is uncomfortable or unsure about something?

a) They will tell you directly

b) They will seem nervous or hesitant

c) They will say "maybe" or "I'm not sure"

5. What is a boundary?

a) A physical line in the sand

b) A limit someone sets for themselves about what they're comfortable with

c) Something you can cross if you're really determined

Answers:

1. b) When someone agrees to something of their own free will

2. b) No, never

3. b) Respect their decision and find something else to do

4. b) They will seem nervous or hesitant

5. b) A limit someone sets for themselves about what they're comfortable with

Dealing with conflict in relationships

When we build relationships with others, there may come a time when we experience conflict.

When we disagree with someone, when someone harms us or when we hurt someone else, or when we have opposing wants or needs, conflict can arise. It can be unpleasant, but it is a typical part of any relationship.

Conflict, on the other hand, does not have to be a bad thing. It's an opportunity to learn how to communicate effectively, comprehend each other's points of view, and come up with a solution that works for everyone.

Using "I" statements to resolve dispute is one method. Instead of blaming or pointing fingers, we can discuss how we feel and what we desire.

Instead of stating, "You're always ignoring me," we should say, "I feel ignored when you don't listen to me." This prevents the other person from feeling attacked or defensive.

Active listening is another effective method. This is listening to what the other person is saying and attempting to comprehend their point of view.

We can ask questions, repeat what they said to clarify, and demonstrate that we are genuinely interested in understanding where they are coming from.

Finally, we must remember that it is acceptable to differ. We may have opposing viewpoints and beliefs, but we must nonetheless respect each other's boundaries and feelings.

We can collaborate to create a solution on which everyone can agree, or we can agree to differ without inflicting hurt or disrespect to one another.

We can learn to handle disagreements in a healthy and courteous manner by employing these tactics, as well as establish deeper connections with people around us.

Assume you and your best friend have opposing views on anything, such as which superhero is the best. You may adore Spiderman, while your mate regards Batman as far superior.

You and your friend are debating about it one day, and your friend becomes quite upset. He starts yelling and pushing you, and you're at a loss for what to do. You could be terrified, furious, or upset. However, it is critical to realize that fighting and hurting one other is never the solution.

Instead, try to relax by taking a deep breath. Then, attempt to speak things over with your friend quietly.

Even if you disagree with him, listen to what he has to say and try to comprehend his point of view. Also, remember to communicate your own views and opinions without assaulting or hurting your friend.

If you are unable to solve a problem on your own, it is OK to seek assistance from an adult. They may assist you in finding a solution that works for everyone and teaching you how to resolve disagreements in a healthy manner. Remember that it is always preferable to speak things out and work together to find a solution rather than harming each other and create more difficulties.

CHAPTER FOUR

Navigating Gender and Sexual Identity

Gender and sexual identity can be a difficult subject to navigate, but it's vital to remember that it's normal to explore and discover who you are.

Everyone is unique and wonderful, and your gender and sexual orientation are part of that.

Gender identification refers to whether you identify more as a boy, a girl, or something in between. Sexual identity refers to who you are attracted to, whether it be boys, girls, or both.

It's crucial to remember that everyone's gender and sexual identity is unique, and it's perfectly fine to experiment and discover out what you're most comfortable with. It is critical to be respectful of individuals and their identities.

Assume your friend Johnny informs you that he identifies as genderqueer, which means they do not fit into the traditional definitions of male or female. Instead of mocking or dismissing what they've stated, it's critical to listen to and encourage them.

It's also critical to recognize that your gender and sexual identity can shift and evolve over time. You may feel one way right now, but as you grow and learn more about yourself, you may uncover other aspects of yourself that you were unaware of.

Remember that figuring out your gender and sexual identity is a journey, and it's good to take your time. Don't be afraid to seek answers or advice from reliable adults or friends.

It is critical to respect oneself and others, as well as to be kind and empathetic at all times.

Everyone, no matter who they are or who they love, deserves to be treated with love and respect.

Understanding gender and gender expression

Let's go on an adventure into the realm of gender and gender expression! Consider yourself traveling through a crowded street fair full with people from various walks of life.

As you make your way through the crowd, you realize that not everyone looks or dresses alike. Some people have short hair, while others have long hair or brilliantly colored hair.

Some people are dressed in dresses or skirts, whereas others are dressed in slacks or shorts. Some people have a lower-pitched voice, while others have a higher-pitched voice.

But here's the thing: none of these distinctions have any bearing on who these folks are as persons.

Gender expression, like the unique traits that distinguish each person's face, is a method for people to express themselves in a way that feels authentic to who they are. And, just as some people have blue eyes or brown hair, others feel more at ease expressing themselves in ways that defy traditional gender conventions.

For some people, the gender assigned to them at birth (typically based on their physical anatomy) does not correspond to how they feel on the inside.

This is referred to as gender identity. Some people feel that their gender identity does not fit with what society expects of them based on their biological sex, just as you may feel that you prefer dogs to cats.

It is critical to recognize that gender identity and expression are highly personal and unique to each individual. They are not influenced by the views or opinions of others.

That is why we must recognize and support people's gender identities and expressions, even when they differ from our own.

What about sexual orientation, though? This refers to who we are emotionally, romantically, or sexually attracted to. It is critical to understand that gender identity and expression are distinct from sexual orientation.

Just as you may be drawn to persons of a given gender, someone's gender identity or expression does not determine who they are drawn to.

We can make the world a more inclusive and accepting place by understanding more about gender and gender expression. So, let us appreciate our uniqueness and what makes each of us distinct.

!

Different sexual orientations and identities

Things might become a little complicated when it comes to sexual orientation and identity. But don't worry, we're here to help make sense of it all!

A person's sexual orientation refers to their emotional, romantic, or sexual attraction to another. There are numerous sexual orientations, and each person's experience is unique.

Some people are drawn to people of the opposite gender, while others are drawn to people of the same gender and still others to people of several genders. It's critical to remember that all sexual orientations are legitimate and normal.

Gender identity is a person's internal sense of their own gender, which may differ from the gender given to them at birth. Similarly, there are other gender identities other than male and female.

Some people identify as non-binary or gender non-conforming, which means they do not fit into established gender roles. Again, keep in mind that everyone's experience is valid and normal.

So, let's look at some of the most frequent sexual orientations and gender identities:

Heterosexual: This refers to someone who is attracted to people of the opposite gender.

Homosexual: This refers to someone who is attracted to people of the same gender.

Bisexual: This refers to someone who is attracted to people of both the same and opposite gender.

Pansexual: This refers to someone who is attracted to people regardless of their gender.

Asexual: This refers to someone who doesn't experience sexual attraction.

Demisexual: This refers to someone who only experiences sexual attraction after forming a strong emotional bond with someone.

Queer: This is a term that some people use to describe their sexuality or gender identity when they don't fit into traditional categories.

Non-binary: This refers to someone who doesn't identify as exclusively male or female.

Transgender: This refers to someone whose gender identity differs from the gender they were assigned at birth.

Genderfluid: This refers to someone whose gender identity changes over time.

Remember that these are just a few of the numerous sexual orientations and gender identities that exist.

It's fine if you're not sure which label best describes you or if none of them seem to apply to you. The most essential thing is to be true to oneself while still respecting the identities and experiences of others.

It's also vital to remember that everyone, regardless of sexual orientation or gender identity, deserves love, respect, and support.

There are resources and support available if you or someone you know is dealing with their identity. If you need assistance, don't be hesitant to ask for it.

Consider the following scenario: you are at school and notice a boy who has a crush on another boy in your class. Perhaps you've heard other kids make fun of him for it.

But keep in mind that having affections for anyone, regardless of gender, is acceptable.

Assume you have a friend who has feelings for a girl in your class. You can let your friend understand that making fun of someone for preferring someone of the same gender is not acceptable.

You can also remind them that everyone, regardless of who they prefer, deserves respect.

Another scenario is if a family member or acquaintance comes out to you as gay, lesbian, bisexual, or any other sexual orientation.

It may be difficult to grasp at first, but it is critical to support them and treat them with dignity.

You might ask them questions to better understand their experiences and assure them that you love and accept them regardless of their circumstances.

Remember that everyone, regardless of sexual orientation or gender identity, deserves to feel accepted and appreciated for who they are. You can make a significant difference in someone's life by being a helpful and understanding friend or family member.

Understanding and respecting different sexual orientations and gender identities is an important step toward making the world more inclusive and tolerant.

We can help break down negative preconceptions and create a safer and more inclusive neighborhood for everyone by educating ourselves and others.

Supporting friends who identify differently than you

Supporting your friends is an important part of any friendship. And sometimes, supporting your friends means being there for them when they are going through a tough time.

If your friend identifies differently than you do, it's important to be there for them, no matter what.

Here are some things you can do to support your friend:

Listen: Sometimes all someone needs is someone to listen to them. If your friend is going through a tough time, take the time to listen to them. Ask them how they are feeling and be there for them.

Ask Questions: If you're not sure how to support your friend, ask them! They might have some ideas on what they need.

It's okay to not know everything, and asking questions is a great way to show your friend that you care.

Educate Yourself: If your friend identifies differently than you do, take the time to educate yourself about their identity.

Read books or watch movies with characters who identify similarly to your friend. This will help you understand their perspective and give you more ideas on how to support them.

Respect Boundaries: Everyone has boundaries, and it's important to respect them. If your friend doesn't want to talk about their identity or doesn't want to participate in certain activities, respect their decision.

Stand Up for Them: If you hear someone making fun of your friend or saying hurtful things, speak up. Let them know that it's not okay to say things like that and that your friend deserves respect.

Remember, supporting your friend is all about being there for them and showing them that you care. By doing these things, you can make a big difference in their life and show them that they are not alone.

Dealing with bullying and discrimination

Consider the following scenario: You're strolling down the corridor at school, minding your own business, when you overhear someone making fun of one of your classmates.

You notice a group of older students calling your friend names and making fun of the way she dresses.

You become irritated and frustrated, but you don't know what to do. You understand that such behavior is unacceptable, but you also don't want to make matters worse for your friend.

Many children have been in this predicament at some point in their lives. It's difficult to know how to respond when you witness bullying or discrimination. But keep in mind that there are things you may do to aid.

First, make sure your pal is all right. Inquire whether they require assistance or support. Knowing that someone cares can make all the difference in the world.

Next, try to talk to the person who is bullying or discriminating against you. It's critical to approach them calmly and respectfully.

"Hey, I don't think it's cool to make fun of someone like that," you could say. It is not acceptable to be cruel to others."

It's okay to move away and seek help from a trusted adult, such as a teacher or counselor, if the person doesn't listen or continues to be hurtful. They can assist you in developing a strategy to deal with the circumstance.

It's also crucial to understand that bullying and bigotry can manifest themselves in a variety of ways. It is not necessarily visible or physical.

It can also be subtle, such as removing someone from a group or making fun of their interests. When you witness any type of damaging activity, it is critical that you speak up.

Remember that everyone deserves to be treated with dignity and respect. You may make a difference in someone's life and help create a safer, more inclusive environment for all by speaking out against bullying and prejudice.

Quiz Time

1. What is bullying?

a. When someone takes your lunch money

b. When someone repeatedly hurts, threatens or intimidates you on purpose

c. When someone accidentally bumps into you

2. What are some types of bullying?

 a. Physical, verbal and cyber

b. Emotional, musical and environmental

c. Intellectual, musical and linguistic

3. Who can you talk to if you are being bullied?

a. Your friends who are also being bullied

b. Your parents, teachers or a trusted adult

c. No one, you have to handle it yourself

4. What is discrimination?

a. Treating someone differently because of their race, gender, religion or other personal characteristics

b. Not liking someone because of their haircut

c. Ignoring someone because they don't like the same sports as you

5. How can you be an ally to someone who is being discriminated against?

a. Stand up for them, speak out against discrimination and support them

b. Join in with the discrimination so you can fit in with the crowd
c. Ignore the discrimination and hope it goes away

Answers:

1. b,

2. a,

3. b,

4. a,

5. a

CHAPTER FIVE

The Word SEX and Good Hygiene

Let's discuss how to keep safe and healthy, boys! Taking good care of our bodies and maintaining appropriate cleanliness is a crucial component of it.

That entails taking regular showers, brushing our teeth, and dressing in spick-and-span. Even though it might not seem important, taking care of ourselves keeps us healthy and makes us feel good.

Safe sex practices are another crucial aspect of maintaining good health. You may be asking yourself, "But I'm not having sex yet, why do I need to know about this?"

Well, being organized and knowledgeable is always a good idea! Furthermore, learning how to protect ourselves and others safe should never start too early.

Let's first discuss what safe sex entails. Safe sex is taking precautions to avoid unintended pregnancy and sexually transmitted infections (STIs).

This could entail using a condom when having sex or visiting the doctor frequently to ensure our health.

I am aware that discussing sex can be uncomfortable or embarrassing. But it's crucial to keep in mind that there's nothing wrong with having inquiries or a desire to find out more. It's both healthy and absolutely normal. You can search for information online from a reliable source or speak with a trusted adult, such as a parent or doctor.

It's crucial to keep in mind that sexual activity should always be consent-based. That calls for a complete and passionate acceptance of the situation from all parties.

Nobody should ever feel coerced or forced into doing something they don't want to. Always stop and inquire if you're unsure if someone is giving their consent.

Keep in mind that practicing safe sex and taking care of our bodies are crucial components of developing into healthy adults. Let's all do our part to maintain the health and safety of our communities and ourselves!

Sex and the meaning

Sex is a term used to describe how babies are made. When a sperm from a man's body meets an egg from a woman's body, it can grow into a baby.

This usually happens when a man and a woman have sexual intercourse, which is when the man's penis enters the woman's vagina.

But it's important to remember that sex can mean different things to different people and can happen in different ways, including between people of the same gender.

It's also important to know that not all sexual activity leads to pregnancy, and that there are many ways to be intimate with someone that don't involve sex. For example, hugging, holding hands, and kissing are all ways to show affection without having sex.

With that in mind, let's talk about practicing safe sex and hygiene!

The importance of hygiene
Maintaining health and feeling good about ourselves require good cleanliness.

By taking care of our bodies, we lower our risk of being sick and experience more self-assurance and comfort.

Let's begin with the fundamentals. Simple self-care and cleanliness are the foundation of hygiene. This entails doing regular hand washing, bathing or showering, brushing your teeth twice daily, and dressing in clean clothes.

Washing your hands frequently is one of the most crucial things you can do to keep yourself healthy.

Prior to eating, after using the restroom, after petting pets, and after blowing your nose, sneezing, or coughing, wash your hands.

Scrub your hands for at least 20 seconds with soap and warm water, then thoroughly rinse and dry them.

Keeping your body clean also involves bathing or taking a shower. To clean your skin and hair, use soap and shampoo.

Even while you don't have to take a shower or bath every day, it's a good idea to do so at least a few times per week, particularly if you exercise frequently or perspire a lot.

Another crucial aspect of hygiene is brushing your teeth. Two minutes should be spent brushing your teeth each time, twice a day. Make sure to brush your tongue and all the surfaces of your teeth using a soft-bristled brush and fluoride-containing toothpaste.

For proper hygiene, it's also crucial to dress neatly. Although you don't have to change into new clothes every day, you should if they become soiled or sweaty. Wash your garments frequently, paying specific attention to your socks and underwear.

You can take care of your body by doing a few extra things in addition to these fundamental hygiene procedures. To keep your nails clean and free from infections, trim them frequently.

To avoid body odor, use antiperspirant or deodorant. Additionally, if you have acne, wash your face frequently and follow the directions on the acne medications you use.

You can take care of yourself, feel good about yourself, and stay healthy by maintaining good hygiene. It's crucial to incorporate these routines into your everyday life and to maintain them.

And never be reluctant to speak with a responsible adult or a healthcare professional if you ever have questions or concerns regarding personal hygiene or your health.

Imagine you and your pals are at a basketball game. You're having a fantastic time supporting your favorite team and giving your friends high fives whenever they say something insightful. However, you soon become aware of how sweaty and unpleasant your hands are feeling.

You run the risk of spreading germs and getting sick both yourself and others if you frequently touch your face, your friends' hands, or anything else nearby.

It is crucial to maintain proper hygiene practices, such as routine hand washing, especially before handling food or your face.

Another illustration is when you're playing in the mud and dirt outside. Although being dirty is a lot of fun, improper cleanup might make you ill. If you don't thoroughly wash your hands and body after playing outside, you could develop an uncomfortable rash or possibly an illness.

In addition to keeping yourself clean and healthy, hygiene also has to do with how you feel about yourself. You feel more confident and prepared to take on the day when you are tidy and well-groomed. Additionally, it's a method to respect both yourself and those around you.

STI's and how to prevent them

Hey there, boys! You've probably heard the term "STI" before, but do you know what it means? STI stands for "sexually transmitted infection," which is an infection that can be passed from one person to another during sexual activity. There are many different types of STIs, and they can affect both boys and girls.

Some common STIs include chlamydia, gonorrhea, genital herpes, HPV (human papillomavirus), and HIV (human immunodeficiency virus). STIs can have serious health consequences if left untreated, so it's important to take steps to prevent them.

One of the most effective ways to prevent STIs is by practicing safe sex abstinence from sex. This means using a barrier method, like a condom or dental dam, during sexual activity.

Condoms are a type of barrier method that fit over the penis and can help prevent the spread of STIs. Dental dams are a thin sheet of latex or polyurethane that can be placed over the anus or vulva during oral sex.

It's important to use condoms and dental dams correctly to ensure that they work effectively. Make sure to read the instructions carefully and ask an adult or a trusted healthcare provider if you have any questions.

Another way to prevent STIs is by getting vaccinated. The HPV vaccine is recommended for both boys and girls between the ages of 9 and 12, and can help protect against several types of HPV that can cause cancer.

Practicing good hygiene is also important in preventing the spread of STIs. Make sure to wash your hands regularly, especially before and after touching your genitals. It's also a good idea to shower or bathe regularly, especially after sexual activity.

There is time for everything

Let's talk about something important: sex. You might have heard about it from friends or seen it on TV, but do you really know what it means?

Sex is when two people have intimate contact, usually involving their private parts. It's a big decision to make, and one that should only be made when you are ready.

So, why wait? There are many reasons why you might want to wait until you are older and more mature before having sex. For one thing, it's a big responsibility.

You need to be emotionally and physically ready to handle the consequences that come with sex, like pregnancy or sexually transmitted infections (STIs).

Also, sex is something that should only be done with someone you trust and respect. If you're not in a committed, loving relationship with someone, it can lead to feelings of regret and hurt.

Now, let's talk about how you can stay away from sex until you're ready. The best way to do this is by practicing abstinence, which means choosing not to have sex at all. This might sound difficult, but it's actually a great way to protect yourself from unwanted consequences.

Here are some tips for staying abstinent:

Know your boundaries: It's important to know what you're comfortable with and what you're not. Think about what your values are and what you want out of a relationship.

Stay true to yourself: Don't let peer pressure or popular culture influence your decisions about sex. Remember, it's okay to say "no" if you're not ready.

Set boundaries with your partner: If you're in a relationship, make sure you communicate your boundaries with your partner. Let them know what you're comfortable with and what you're not.

Practice safe behaviors: Even if you're not having sex, it's important to practice safe behaviors to prevent STIs.

This includes using protection during any type of sexual contact and getting regular check-ups with your doctor.

Remember, it's okay to wait until you're ready to have sex. By practicing abstinence and staying true to yourself, you're making a responsible decision that will benefit you in the long run.

CHAPTER SIX

Media and Internet Literacy

Have you ever heard the phrase "Don't believe everything you read on the internet"? Well, it's true! Not everything you see or read online is true or accurate. It's important to be aware of this and learn how to be a smart and critical consumer of online media.

Media literacy is the ability to understand and analyze the messages you see and hear in media, such as on TV, in movies, and on the internet.

It's important to develop media literacy skills so that you can recognize and understand the messages you are receiving, and make informed decisions about what to believe and how to act.

The internet is an amazing tool that can be used for learning, connecting with friends, and having fun. But there are also risks and dangers associated with being online, such as cyberbullying, scams, and inappropriate content.

That's why it's important to develop internet literacy skills, such as being able to identify fake news, protect your personal information, and navigate online safely.

Here are some tips for being a smart and responsible media and internet user:

Be critical of what you see and read online. Not everything you see is true or accurate. Always check your sources before sharing or believing something.

Ensure the privacy of your personal data. Without the consent of an adult you can trust, never provide your name, address, phone number, or other personal information online.

Make sure your passwords are secure and confidential. Useless passwords like "123456" or "password" should be avoided. And never, not even with your buddies, divulge your password.

When communicating with strangers online, use caution. Never exchange private information or meet up with strangers in person.

Online respect towards others. Don't share or publish offensive content, and don't bully or harass others.

Don't stare at the screen for too long. Taking breaks to engage in different hobbies, like reading, playing sports, or spending time with family and friends, is crucial.

You can utilize online media in an intelligent and responsible way by learning media and internet literacy skills. Therefore, always exercise caution when viewing or reading content online, safeguard your personal information, and show consideration for others.

Quiz Time

1 .What is media literacy?

A) Understanding and analyzing media messages

B) Knowing how to use different types of media devices

C) Being able to create your own media content

2. What is cyberbullying?

A) Making fun of someone in person

B) Sending mean or hurtful messages online

C) Arguing with someone in an online game

3. What is the purpose of fact-checking information?

A) To make sure it is accurate and true

B) To see if it agrees with your personal opinions

C) To make sure it is interesting and engaging

3. What is online privacy?

A) Keeping your personal information safe online

B) Sharing your personal information with strangers online

C) Creating fake profiles to hide your identity online

4. What is the purpose of a copyright law?

A) To protect someone's original work from being used without permission

B) To allow people to use any information they find online

C) To make sure everyone can see and use any information they want

Answers:

1. A
2. B
3. A
4. A
5. A

Understanding media messages about sex

Media plays a big role in our lives. It's everywhere we look, from TV shows to social media to advertisements.

But have you ever thought about the messages that media sends about sex?

It's important to understand these messages so that you can make informed decisions about your own sexual health.

One message that media often sends about sex is that it's something that everyone is doing. You might see TV shows or movies where characters are having sex casually or even just hooking up with strangers.

But the truth is that not everyone is having sex, and it's okay if you're not ready or interested in it yet.

Another message that media sends about sex is that it's always easy and enjoyable. In reality, sex can be complicated and messy, and it's important to make sure that you're ready and willing before engaging in any sexual activity.

It's also important to understand that media often portrays sex in a way that's not always realistic or healthy. For example, you might see portrayals of sex that involve coercion, pressure, or even violence. These types of behaviors are not acceptable and can lead to physical and emotional harm.

So how can you be media literate when it comes to sex? Here are a few tips:

Question what you see: Whenever you see a message about sex in the media, ask yourself if it's realistic or healthy. Don't believe everything you see on TV or social media.

Talk to someone you trust: If you're unsure about a message you've seen, talk to a trusted adult or friend. They can help you understand it better and provide guidance.

Educate yourself: Learn about healthy relationships, consent, and safe sex practices. This knowledge will help you make informed decisions when it comes to your own sexual health.

Here's a short story example that illustrates how to apply critical thinking skills when consuming media messages about sex:

Once upon a time, there was a boy named Jack who loved watching movies about superheroes. One day, Jack saw a trailer for a new movie that he thought looked really cool.

The movie was about a superhero who had the power to seduce anyone he wanted with just a look. Jack was excited to see the movie, but he also felt a little confused. He knew that seducing someone without their consent was wrong, but the movie made it seem like it was a good thing.

Jack decided to talk to his older sister about it. She told him that it was important to think critically about the messages we receive from media. Just because something is portrayed in a movie or on TV doesn't mean it's okay in real life. She suggested that Jack ask himself some questions to help him better understand the message of the movie:

What is the movie trying to tell me about the superhero's power?

How does the movie portray the people who are being seduced?

Does the movie make it clear whether or not the people being seduced are consenting to it?

What are the potential consequences of using this power?

Jack thought about his sister's questions and realized that the movie wasn't just about a cool superhero power, but about the importance of consent and respecting other people's boundaries.

He decided that if he did watch the movie, he would do so with a critical eye and think about the underlying messages.

This story shows how a young boy can use critical thinking skills to understand the messages presented in media about sex. It encourages boys to be aware of the messages they are receiving and to question whether or not those messages align with their own values and beliefs.

Identifying harmful or unrealistic messages

When we watch TV, go on social media or play video games, we are exposed to a lot of different messages. Sometimes these messages can be helpful, like when we learn something new or see someone doing a good deed. But other times, these messages can be harmful or unrealistic. They can make us feel bad about ourselves or our bodies, or make us believe things that aren't true.

So, how do we identify these harmful or unrealistic messages? Here are some tips:

Be aware of the messages you are receiving.

When you're watching TV or playing a game, pay attention to the messages you're seeing and hearing. Ask yourself: what is this message saying? Is it true? Does it make me feel good about myself? If the message is harmful or unrealistic, try to turn it off or change the channel.

Look for positive role models.

Instead of focusing on negative messages, look for positive role models. These can be people you know in real life, or people you see in movies or on TV. Look for people who are kind, brave, and who treat others with respect. These are the kinds of messages that will make you feel good about yourself and the world around you.

Talk to someone you trust.

If you're not sure if a message is harmful or unrealistic, talk to someone you trust. This could be a parent, teacher, or friend. They can help you understand the message and give you advice on how to handle it.

Remember that not everything you see is real.

Just because something is on TV or social media, doesn't mean it's real. A lot of times, things are edited or staged to look a certain way. It's important to remember that what you see on the screen may not be the whole story.

By following these tips, you can learn to identify harmful or unrealistic messages and protect yourself from their negative effects.

Remember, it's important to be mindful of the messages you're receiving and to always look for positive role models.

Staying safe online

As a young boy growing up in the digital age, you have access to a wealth of information, entertainment, and communication tools online.

While this can be incredibly beneficial, it can also present some dangers. It's important to know how to stay safe and healthy online.

One of the first things you need to do to stay safe online is to protect your personal information. This includes your name, address, phone number, and any other details that could be used to identify you.

Additionally, you should exercise caution while posting images and videos online because they could be used to locate you or damage your reputation.

Using strong passwords and protecting your accounts are two additional crucial aspects of remaining secure and healthy online. Your passwords should never be disclosed to anyone, and you should make sure they are challenging to crack.

Additionally, you should be cautious about the websites you visit and the links you click on since some of them may include viruses or malware that can damage your computer or steal your personal information.

It's also critical to be mindful of the dangers posed by conversations conducted online.

Social media and other online platforms can be excellent for maintaining relationships with friends and family, but they can also be used to abuse, harass, or manipulate other people.

You should use caution in your online behavior and always show respect for others.

Here are tips you need:

Use Strong and Unique Passwords

One of the easiest ways to protect yourself online is to use strong and unique passwords for all your accounts. A strong password should be at least eight characters long and include a mix of uppercase and lowercase letters, numbers, and special characters.

Also, avoid using the same password for multiple accounts, as this makes it easier for hackers to gain access to all your accounts if they manage to guess your password for one of them.

Keep Your Personal Information Private

Never share your personal information, such as your full name, address, phone number, or social security number, online.

This information can be used by cybercriminals to steal your identity or commit other types of fraud. Be careful when sharing your location or photos online, as this can also put your safety at risk.

Be Careful When Downloading Files

Be cautious when downloading files from the internet, as they can contain viruses or malware that can harm your computer or steal your personal information.

Only download files from reputable sources, and make sure you have a good antivirus program installed on your computer to protect against threats.

Don't Believe Everything You See Online

Just because something is posted on the internet doesn't mean it's true. Be skeptical of news stories, advertisements, and other online content that seems too good to be true or is trying to sell you something.

Use your critical thinking skills to evaluate the information you see online and do your own research before believing or sharing anything.

Be Respectful of Others

Remember that there are real people on the other end of the screen, and treat them with the same respect you would in person. Avoid cyberbullying, harassment, and hate speech, and report any inappropriate behavior you encounter online.

Take Breaks and Stay Active

Spending too much time online can be bad for your mental and physical health. Take regular breaks to stretch, exercise, or spend time outdoors. It's also important to get enough sleep and to limit your screen time before bed to help you sleep better.

Finally, it's important to maintain a healthy balance between your online and offline activities. Spending too much time online can be harmful to your physical and mental health, as well as your relationships with others.

You should try to limit your screen time and engage in other activities, such as sports, hobbies, or spending time with friends and family.

By following these tips, you can stay safe and healthy online. Remember that the internet can be a powerful tool, but it's up to you to use it responsibly.

QUIZ TIME

1. *What is personal information?*

a. Information that belongs to someone else

b. Information about yourself that can identify you

c. Information that is not important

2. *Why is it important to keep personal information private online?*

a. To protect your privacy and safety

b. To make new friends

c. To impress others

3. *What should you do if you receive a message from a stranger online?*

a. Reply to the message and start a conversation

b. Ignore the message and delete it

c. Reply to the message and share personal information

4. *What is cyberbullying?*

a. A type of bullying that occurs online

b. A type of bullying that only occurs in person

c. A type of bullying that doesn't exist

5. *What should you do if you are being cyberbullied?*

a. Respond with mean messages to defend yourself

b. Tell an adult you trust and report the incident

c. Delete all your social media accounts

6. *What is a virus?*

a. A type of bacteria

b. A type of software that can harm your computer

c. A type of animal

7. *How can you protect yourself from viruses?*

a. Only visit trusted websites and download files from trusted sources

b. Share your personal information with everyone online

c. Click on every link and download every file you come across

8. *What is phishing?*

a. A type of fishing

b. A type of scam that uses emails or other messages to trick people into giving out personal information

c. A type of computer game

9. What should you do if you receive a suspicious email or message?

a. Click on the links and follow the instructions

b. Ignore the message and delete it

c. Forward the message to all your friends

10. What is two-factor authentication?

a. A type of password that is easy to guess

b. A security feature that requires two forms of identification to access an account

c. A type of social media platform

Answers:

1. b
2. a
3. b
4. a
5. b
6. b
7. a
8. b
9. b
10. b

Story Time

Once upon a time, there was a boy named Max who loved playing video games. He loved talking to other gamers online and sharing his gaming experiences with them.

However, one day he received a friend request from a stranger who claimed to be a fellow gamer. Max was excited to make a new friend, so he accepted the request without thinking twice.

The stranger started sending Max messages asking for his personal information like his name, address, and phone number. Max got scared and didn't know what to do.

He thought about blocking the stranger but was afraid of hurting his feelings. He also worried that if he didn't reply, the stranger might start harassing him.

Fortunately, Max had learned about staying safe online in school. He remembered that it's never safe to share personal information with strangers online, and that he should always tell a trusted adult if he feels uncomfortable.

So Max decided to talk to his parents about what happened. They were proud of him for being responsible and told him that he did the right thing.

They helped Max report the stranger to the online platform, and they also blocked him from Max's account. Max felt relieved and learned an important lesson about staying safe online.

The moral of the story is that it's essential to be careful and stay safe online. Never share personal information with strangers and always talk to a trusted adult if you feel uncomfortable.

The risks and consequences of sexting and sharing sexual content

Sending or receiving sexually explicit texts, images, or videos via electronic devices such smartphones, tablets, or laptops is known as sexting.

Even though it could seem like a sweet way to flirt or show affection, it can also have negative effects. In this section, we'll talk about the dangers and repercussions of sexting, sharing sexual content, and being a responsible online lad.

Let's start by discussing the dangers. A boy has no control over a sexually explicit message or image once he sends or receives it. He has no means of knowing where it might end up after it is despatched.

The recipient might distribute it or publish it online, which could result in humiliation, harassment, or even blackmail.

Even if he is the one in the picture, the boy may occasionally be subject to legal repercussions, such as being prosecuted with disseminating child pornography.

Sexting and distributing sexual content can have disastrous repercussions. Sexting boys may experience anxiety, depression, or other mental health problems.

Additionally, they could experience social repercussions like bullying or exclusion from their peers. Sexting can seriously affect a boy's relationships, academic performance, and future employment opportunities.

How therefore can boys behave responsibly and safely online? The first step is to refrain from using sexting at all costs.

A boy should delete any sexually explicit messages or images as soon as he sees them and tell an adult he can trust what happened.

Before posting any private information or photographs online, boys should use caution and never post anything they wouldn't want their parents, instructors, or potential employers to view.

Knowing the rules and laws governing sexting and distributing sexual content is an additional crucial step. Boys need to know that it's against the law to distribute sexually explicit material with children, regardless of their ages.

They should also be advised that, even if they are of legal age to consent, sharing explicit material without the other person's consent constitutes an invasion of their privacy and may be illegal.

And finally, guys must maintain decent digital hygiene. When providing personal information online, such as their complete name, address, or phone number, they should use secure passwords.

Additionally, kids need to exercise caution when using applications and websites, making sure to read and comprehend the terms of service and privacy policies before registering.

Chapter Seven

Answering Common Questions about Sex and Relationships

What is sex?

A: Sex is when two grown up people's private parts come together to create a special kind of feeling. It's how people make babies, there are a lot of consequences and other bad stuffs that can happen if sex is done before the right time.

How can I tell if someone likes me?

A: Sometimes it can be hard to tell if someone likes you, but some signs include: they want to spend time with you, they make an effort to talk to you, they may tease you in a playful way, and they might give you compliments.

What should I do if someone is making me feel uncomfortable?

A: If someone is making you feel uncomfortable or unsafe, it's important to tell a trusted adult like a parent or teacher. You have the right to feel safe and respected, and it's okay to ask for help if you need it.

Why do people break up?

A: People break up for many different reasons. Sometimes they grow apart, have different goals or interests, or they might realize that they're not compatible. It's okay to end a relationship if it's not making you happy or if you're not getting what you need from it.

How can I be a good friend?

A: Being a good friend means being kind, respectful, and supportive. It's important to listen to your friends, be there for them when they need you, and treat them the way you would want to be treated.

What if I have a crush on someone who doesn't like me back?

A: It's normal to have feelings for someone who may not feel the same way about you. It's important to respect their feelings and understand that not everyone will be interested in us in the same way we're interested in them.

Focus on building strong friendships and being yourself, and you might find that someone who likes you for who you are will come along.

How can I tell if someone likes me?

A: It can be tricky to know if someone likes you, but here are some signs to look out for: they pay extra attention to you, they try to be near you often, they ask you questions about yourself, and they smile and laugh at your jokes.

Keep in mind that not everyone shows their interest in the same way, so it's always a good idea to communicate and ask someone directly if you're unsure.

What should I do if someone is bullying me?

A: If someone is bullying you, it's important to tell a trusted adult, like a teacher or parent. They can help you come up with a plan to stay safe and address the situation. It's also important to remember that bullying is never your fault and you deserve to be treated with respect and kindness.

What should I do if I'm feeling left out or lonely?

A: It's normal to feel left out or lonely sometimes, but there are things you can do to feel better. Try reaching out to a friend or family member and talk to them about how you're feeling.

You could also try joining a club or activity that interests you to meet new people who share your interests. Remember, everyone feels left out or lonely sometimes, and it's okay to ask for help or support when you need it.

What does it mean to be in a healthy relationship?

A: A healthy relationship means that both people feel respected, supported, and happy. It's important to communicate openly and honestly with each other, listen to each other's needs, and respect each other's boundaries.

In a healthy relationship, both people should feel safe, secure, and able to be themselves around each other. If you ever feel uncomfortable or unsafe in a relationship, it's important to talk to a trusted adult and seek help

How does a baby grow in the mom's belly?

A: When a woman becomes pregnant, a fertilized egg attaches to the lining of her uterus, and starts to grow into a baby. Over time, the baby grows bigger and bigger, until it's ready to be born.

How does the baby come out of the mom's belly?

A: When the baby is ready to be born, the mom's body goes into labor. This means her uterus starts to tighten and push the baby down towards the birth canal.

When the baby is at the bottom of the birth canal, the mom pushes to help the baby come out. The baby usually comes out head first, and then the rest of its body follows.

Does it hurt for the mom to give birth?

A: Yes, giving birth can be painful for the mom. But there are ways to manage the pain, such as medication, breathing techniques, and support from a doctor or midwife.

How long does it take for a baby to be born?

A: The length of time it takes for a baby to be born varies from woman to woman and from baby to baby. For some women, labor and delivery can last just a few hours, while for others it can take many hours or even days.

Can dads be in the room when the baby is born?

A: Yes, many dads choose to be in the room when their baby is born. It can be a very special and emotional experience to witness the birth of your child.

Q: What is a c-section?

A: A c-section, or cesarean section, is a type of surgery where the baby is delivered through a cut in the mom's belly and uterus. It is usually done when there are complications during labor, or when a vaginal birth is not possible or safe for the mom or baby.

Can a mom have more than one baby at a time?

A: Yes, sometimes a mom can have more than one baby at a time. This is called a multiple birth, and it can happen when the mom releases more than one egg at a time, or when a fertilized egg splits into two or more embryos. Twins, triplets, and even higher multiples are possible.

What are the risks of having sex?

A: There are many risks associated with having sex, including the risk of sexually transmitted infections (STIs) and unintended pregnancy.

It's important to use protection, such as condoms or birth control, to reduce these risks. It's also important to make sure you are emotionally ready and comfortable with the decision to have sex.

Providing accurate information to help boys make informed decisions

Sexuality is an important and natural part of human life, and it's normal for boys your age to start having questions and curiosity about it.

It's essential to understand that sex is not only about physical pleasure, but it can also have emotional and mental consequences. That's why it's crucial to have accurate information that can help you make informed decisions.

Here are some important facts to keep in mind:

Consent is essential: Sexual activity should always involve mutual consent between partners. You should never feel pressured or forced to engage in any sexual activity.

Protection is important: Using protection like condoms can reduce the risk of sexually transmitted infections (STIs) and unwanted pregnancy. It's always a good idea to talk to your partner about protection before engaging in sexual activity.

You have the right to say no: If you're not ready for sexual activity or don't feel comfortable, you have the right to say no. It's essential to communicate your feelings with your partner and understand that it's okay to wait until you're ready.

Pornography is not real life: Pornography is often not a realistic depiction of sexual activity and can create unrealistic expectations. It's essential to understand that real-life sex is different from what you may see in videos or pictures.

There's no shame in asking for help: If you have questions or concerns about sexuality, it's okay to reach out to a trusted adult, like a parent, teacher, or doctor. They can provide you with accurate information and support you through any challenges you may face.

Remember, sexuality is a complex topic, and it's essential to have accurate information to make informed decisions. Don't be afraid to ask questions and seek help if you need it. By doing so, you can ensure that you have healthy and safe sexual experiences.

CHAPTER EIGHT

CONCLUSION

As we come to the end of our journey through this book on sex education for boys, it's important to take a moment to recap what we've learned.

Recap of keypoints

We've covered a lot of ground, from the basics of anatomy and puberty to healthy relationships and media literacy. Here are some key points to remember:

- Your body is yours, and it's important to respect yourself and others.
- Puberty is a natural process that happens to everyone, and it's nothing to be ashamed of.
- Sexual feelings are normal, but it's important to make sure any sexual activity is safe, respectful, and consensual.
- Healthy relationships involve communication, respect, and trust.
- Media messages about sex can be confusing and unrealistic, so it's important to think critically about what you see and hear.
- Sexting and sharing sexual content can have serious consequences, so it's important to think twice before engaging in these behaviors.

- There are many myths and misconceptions about sex, and it's important to get accurate information from reliable sources.
- Making informed decisions about sex and relationships involves thinking about your own values and goals, as well as the needs and feelings of others.

Remember, this book is just the beginning. There are many resources available to help you continue learning and growing when it comes to sex education. Talk to trusted adults in your life, like parents, teachers, or doctors, if you have questions or concerns. You can also find reliable information online or in books like this one.

Most importantly, remember that learning about sex and relationships is an ongoing process. You may have questions or concerns at different stages of your life, and that's okay. It's important to keep the lines of communication open and to approach these topics with curiosity, respect, and an open mind.

So, congratulations on making it through this book! We hope you've learned a lot and feel more confident and informed about sex and relationships. Good luck on your journey, and remember to stay safe, respectful, and true to yourself.

Made in United States
North Haven, CT
25 January 2024

47877127R00055